Lisa & Scott
A Tale of Love . . . and Survival

A romantic relationship blossomed late in life for Lisa and Scott some years after both of their long-term and happy marriages abruptly ended when their spouses unexpectedly passed away. This is their story, relived through text messages which they exchanged after meeting at a karaoke session in a Long Island tavern. Lisa's words are italicized to distinguish them from Scott's.

Being private individuals who shun the spotlight, Lisa and Scott were hesitant at first to have their intimate feelings revealed to other people. They finally decided to permit their story to be relived in the pages of this book after realizing that by doing so, other couples might quite possibly be inspired to make every effort to overcome their own stumbling blocks to a lasting relationship which love alone can't always conquer. Readers should also note that to assist in safeguarding their privacy, fictitious names have been given to most of the people and places mentioned in this work, including Lisa and Scott.

LISA & SCOTT

A Tale of Love
. . . and Survival

Compiled and Edited by
Michael Griske

Poetry by Catherine Mayrides
and Michael Griske

HERITAGE BOOKS
2019

HERITAGE BOOKS
AN IMPRINT OF HERITAGE BOOKS, INC.

Books, CDs, and more—Worldwide

For our listing of thousands of titles see our website at
www.HeritageBooks.com

Published 2019 by
HERITAGE BOOKS, INC.
Publishing Division
5810 Ruatan Street
Berwyn Heights, Md. 20740

Copyright © 2019 Catherine Mayrides
and Michael Griske

Heritage Books by the author:

*The Diaries of John Hunton: Made to Last, Written to Last,
Sagas of the Western Frontier*

Lisa & Scott: A Tale of Love ... and Survival

All rights reserved. No part of this book may be reproduced or transmitted in any form or by any means, electronic or mechanical, including photocopying, recording or by any information storage and retrieval system without written permission from the author, except for the inclusion of brief quotations in a review.

International Standard Book Number
Paperbound: 978-0-7884-5901-6

SUMMARY OF CONTENTS

                                                    <u>Page</u>

CHAPTER 1 - *The Beginning of a Second Time Around* . . 3

CHAPTER 2 - *Using the "L" Word for the First Time* 16

CHAPTER 3 - *Two Men in Lisa's Life* 34

CHAPTER 4 - *Navigating Through More Rough Waters* . . 71

CHAPTER 5 - *Another Cliffhanger for the Relationship* . . 95

CHAPTER 6 - *Choosing the Right Path to Follow* 107

                        Embracing Love in the Twilight Years . . . 114

EPILOGUE — *The Key to Staying Alive* 116

SUMMARY OF CONTENTS

Chapter 1

The Beginning of a Second Time Around

* * * * * * *

On Thu, Oct 19, 2017 at 04:52 PM, Lisa wrote:

hi! Would love to get together and talk. Lots to say. Next week pretty busy with grandkids . . . and most likely coming late to McGill's. But just wondering if you have any time this Saturday? If not....another time. If you still want to. Let me know. :) Lisa

Subject: It Was Very Nice
Date: 10/30/17 at 02:42:40 AM

I just got home from Jake's --- no wind nor rain at all along the way --- where I lost about $25. I was up $40 at one point but didn't quit as I should have. Oh, well.

I wanted to tell you again what a great time I had chatting with you and listening to you sing last night. I also wanted to attach my 10 minute play before I forgot that I promised to send you a copy, and I decided to add a document I put together which reflects the opinions of religious and lay people regarding topics we discussed at the first session of the interfaith Bible Study program I mentioned to you. Maybe we can chat about your views on each document if you're at McGill's on Wednesday and have waded through them by that time. And now I'm going to hit the sack.

On Mon, Oct 30, 2017 at 10:54 AM, Lisa wrote:

Thanks for sharing!
Scott...glad you got home safely! I will read what you sent as soon as I get home. You know, Scott, I am so glad we are friends and can talk about anything...and everything! So important. I think we both love and respect honesty. Too much b.s. in the world.
Your friend, L

On Nov 4, 2017 at 10:50 AM, Scott wrote:

Good morning, Lisa ~   I just wanted to tell you what a nice time I had with you last night. I really enjoy your company. You're a great conversationalist --- when we're able to hear each other over the music --- and a very lovely lady. That's a combination which is hard to find.

I hope we'll be getting together again soon, even though you're "somewhat involved" with some other guy. Because of that, it may be a little awkward for me to be as open and flirtatious with you as I've been, but please keep in mind that I'm out of practice in relating on a one-to-one basis to any woman other than my wife. I'm therefore going to leave it up to you to let me know if I'm ever out of line in any way, since I'd hate to lose your companionship and affection because of something that I did or said.

On Sat, Nov 04, 2017 at 12:21 PM, Lisa wrote:

Good morning, Scott!

Was fun last night. One day soon, we need to get together and talk. You have kind of shaken my complacency and forced me to think long and hard

*about my life. In a way, I am glad....and I am certainly glad you are my friend. Scott,
I believe you are sweet and kind .... and soo smart.*

Won't say more. At least right now.

On Sun, Nov 05, 2017 at 11:39 AM, Lisa wrote:

Hi Scott: Since I'm not totally sure about McGill's Weds, would prefer to meet you Thurs am. If I told you all the things that have been floating in and out of my already overcrowded noggin, you may...or may not be surprised. Well, probably not. I overthink things .. and then underthink others....to the point that I'm not trusting myself to make sound decisions. So right now, just putting one foot in front of the other.

We do need to talk .. but maybe it's just ME who needs to talk it out. I have made some awful decisions this year and I'm fully aware of this. There are things I need to UNDO because I'm digging myself into a hole and do not want to be there. I value my freedom and this is not how I want to live.

Life is way too short, something I am hyper-aware of...

Being honest has never been my problem. But you were spot on about this: the 'inferiority' issue..... why do I let certain people 'bully' me in a way that leads me to believe my own opinions could not possibly count?
I know I'm smart. I know I have much to say. And yet, someone with a sad story and murky history can get to me and get me to overlook and excuse bad behaviors???!!!

My mom used to call me the "bleeding heart" and told me to take care of myself first and foremost. I never listened..lil

ok...I can go on and on. But I feel I'm finally coming to terms with things. Will save it all for another time.....

On Nov 9, 2017 at 5:41 PM, Scott wrote:

I just wanted to tell you again what a wonderful time I had today. Thanks so much for spending most of the day with me . . . and for being you. Attached are a couple of shots taken at Cedar

Beach and Mt. Sinai Harbor to help us relive that memorable experience.

There's only one fly in the ointment. I decided to check inside my car again after you left, and I discovered two pieces of your camera equipment on the driver's seat --- the lens cap and a battery charger. I can't imagine how they got there. You probably want them back right away, so if you'd like to hook up with me on Friday at either The Oasis around 9 p.m. or The Beer Hut at 11:00 or so, I can return them to you then. If you won't be coming, I could drop them off at your home on my way to The Oasis, or give them back to you next Wednesday at McGill's. Let me know what you'd like me to do.

Subject: Re: A Great Day.....enjoyed it all! !!!!
Date: 11/09/17 at 06:31:20 PM, Lisa wrote:

oops...didn't know I left stuff in your car. Seems I always leave something behind. I will get it next Weds at McGill's. If I feel ok tomorrow I'll be in Massapequa ....

GREAT day!!! Did I say that already? lol
thanks, Scott...
Your niceness is sweet!!!!!

On Fri, Nov 10, 2017 at 11:07 AM, Lisa wrote:

Always be honest. Tell me if this is not the direction you want to go in.

I hope it is, but .....I've been on earth long enough to know that you can't get what you want every time. But not too cynical to think good things cannot happen. This feels like a good thing.

Subject: RE: *I thought about you first thing this morning. Suddenly, I feel like something's going right. I feel like I can fly.*
I know I am dramatic, lol, but I feel lighter and happier...

On 11/10/17 at 03:47:11 PM, Scott wrote:

I'm so glad it's not only me who feels that way, Lisa. I think about you, as the Cole Porter song says, "Night and Day". Did you know there's a 1940's movie with that title starring Cary Grant? We should watch it sometime.

Anyway, I'll be counting the hours until I see you again. It's going to be hard to wait until Wednesday, but that's the problem in living as far apart as we do as well as having family and personal obligations which take up a good chunk of our time. So until then, just remember what that tune says:

> Whether near to me or far,
> It's no matter, baby, where you are
> I think of you
> Day and night.

I better close for now. I'm starting to get misty.

Subject: RE: hi Scott:
Date: 11/10/17 at 08:47:05 PM

Believe it or not, Lisa, I was just about to send you a message before showering and heading off to The Oasis and The Beer Hut. Since my last email to you vanished, I've inserted it at the end of this one.

First of all, I had a few comments about your email which I've inserted and underlined within your text below. But the reason I was going to send you this message before I got yours was to say that I read your narrative in Sr. Rita's book, and I can see why she included it. The subject matter was not only riveting, but soooo well-written!

I can't wait to read your poetry and other writings. I was very sad, though, when I thought about how you said your parents left you to fend for yourself during childhood, and therefore, their parenting --- or lack thereof --- may have been one of the major root causes of your adopted brother's serious problems. Maybe we can chat more about him sometime.

On Fri, Nov 10, 2017 at 06:50 PM, Lisa wrote:

I went unto my mail to re-read your note ... because it was the sweetest EVER and I wanted to reply...but it seems to have vanished I am sure it's something I did. I need a computer lesson! In any case, it is not something I would forget!
Cole Porter must have been a beautiful soul to think of those words. And you, sending them to me, tells me you are blessed with a gorgeous soul as well.

I hope I can be the person you think I am. Every time you write to me I feel like I'm in top of the world! Wow! What amazing words about me! You're undoubtedly the person who I think you are, and to be worthy of your companionship and affection, I promise to try as hard as I can to live up to those words. Please let me know if you think I'm ever falling short.

Today was a bit upsetting. Argued with Joey, I didn't think he was listening when I said, "it's time to go." It's past time. He says he will pack up Sunday when his son is able to help him. In any case, I am making changes in my life...and feeling good about it. <u>I'm sure that was very hard on both of you, but I definitely think you did the right thing, especially if, in the end, he promised to pack up and leave on Sunday. I hope that comes to pass.</u>

See you soon..... you are special to me! <u>I truly believe that our relationship --- whatever it is now and may grow into if we keep getting together --- is making us both more special to each other, and perhaps to others as well. What a wonderful feeling that is. I seem to have joined you at the top of the world.</u>

<u>You know how much I enjoy the karaoke venues that I go to, so hopefully my taking time out to write this message will give you some indication of how important my communicating with you has become. In fact, it's about 8:45, I haven't showered yet, and I'm going to be so late that I</u>

<u>may just pass on The Oasis tonight and go straight to The Beer Hut. But that's worth it if I can spend time with you, even if it's just on the internet.</u>

On Sun, Nov 12, 2017 at 07:56 PM, Lisa wrote:

o boy. There was one time ...when I realized I cared about you....but felt like I would walk away....and never look back lol....
Lucy and I walked into The Oasis...and I spied you hugging some young chickie...and dancing ....and I thought: I have no right to feel ANY way or other...but I DID! I realize now why. I turned to Lucy and said something like: that's men for ya, all the same! She laughed and I set about ignoring you... which didn't last by the way. It all had something to do with Joey and how he put me into a rotten mood that day...and I was ready to crucify the entire gender.....
But at that moment....I experienced such jealousy...and knew I cared.... surprised??

Subject: Re: Replying to Your Last Message
Date: 11/12/17 at 09:39:14 PM, Scott wrote:

You bet I'm surprised, Lisa . . . surprised that you didn't tell me how you felt earlier. I was attracted to you from the start and wanted to get to know you better, but you were always there chatting and dancing with Lucy and others. And I felt that whenever I tried to get a little "closer", you seemed to be standoffish most of the time, so I really had given up until Lucy stopped coming and you continued to come alone. Thank God you did so we'd be given a chance. I only wish I'd known how you felt sooner.

Just to set the record straight, after my wife passed away and my grief began to subside, I decided that my primary goal in life should be to try to make other people happier. With that in ind, whenever I go to taverns with karaoke or live bands, I chat with people --- especially those who seem to be sad and lonely --- listen to their problems, and occasionally offer advice.

I also serenade women because many of the ones I meet are or have been in a bad relationship or have inattentive men in their lives, and from what I've observed, my paying attention to them in that way almost always lifts their spirits. I can understand how my doing that made you feel like walking away, but now I'm the one who's happy because you didn't, so I'm counting my lucky stars.

Because we're so fond of each other, and may even be more so if we're still together as time goes on, I can stop doing that if you'd like because I don't want to lose what we have. But I'm hoping that you'll agree to let me continue for the sake of the people who seem to benefit from the attention I give them. And even if you say "yes" initially, you can change your mind at any time if it begins to bother you again, even though you know why I'm doing that as well as how I feel about you and what we have. Any thoughts?

Chapter 2

Using the "L" Word for the First Time

* * * * * * *

Subject: Continuing Our Conversations
Date: 11/13/17 at 02:11:27 PM, Scott wrote

Good afternoon, Lisa ~ I'm so happy that you're feeling better, you sweet thing. I've been trying to think of ways to cheer you up, and one thing that came to mind was to send you the attached photo of the sweatshirt I bought today at our local Walmart while I was doing a little shopping there. I think I'm going to wear it to McGill's on Wednesday. I hope that you're feeling well enough by then to be there, too, because although I'd like the sweatshirt to give the other customers an early Christmas chuckle, there's only one woman I'd like to be on that list. In case you haven't guessed who that is, here's a hint . . . her initials are L.J.

I've also attached a photo of me in the Santa suit which I wore while hosting one of my free Christmas karaoke sessions last year in Bohemia. The people there have serious mental and physical conditions (e.g., Downs Syndrome, etc.), but they can still be very perceptive. For example, when I walked into the facility with that Santa suit on, one man said, "*Hi, Scott*", even though the outfit covered just about every part of me except my eyes. The supervisor and I have been laughing about that ever since.

I've inserted some underlined comments into the text of your two emails below. Hope to see you soon.

On Mon, Nov 13, 2017 at 06:55 AM, Lisa wrote:

hi...the night that green evil jealousy surfaced, I was feeling a LOT of things, and for many reasons. And now that I understand you a bit more, I don't want either if us to feel we have to change anything.......

I hope you feel you can be yourself around me! <u>Always.</u> *It's important that I can be MYself around you!* <u>I agree, but again, if anything I do or say bothers you, I'd like you to let me know so that</u>

we can discuss it. We are still discovering new things about each other. So far, I've been delighted with things you reveal about yourself.

Your gregariousness is something I like.....what happened that night was an "aha" moment. I felt something that simultaneously scared me and tickled me: I found I can still FEEL ......

Thank goodness I've reached this age with my capacity to love intact! That's the first time you've used the "L" word, Lisa, when chatting about us. I've been hesitant to use it, but I do love you. I'm just not sure exactly what that means yet, but I'm getting a better idea each time we talk in person or by email . . . and it involves man-to-woman as well as friend-to-friend feelings, I'm happy to say. And when I told you I feel like a kid again.

Subject: Re: One Last Message for Today
Date: 11/13/17 at 12:48:18 PM, Lisa wrote:

The feeling of being 'betwixt and between' and not being sure of where or how to land is intriguing as well....it is feeling more like winter and less like autumn each day.....and the prospect of cold and snow is only overshadowed by the prospect of new beginnings. Of course, I pinch myself and wonder if I dreamed everything that has happened? I hope it is all real! I hope I'm finally the person that good things come to........in the form of a good person who wants to be in my company. You deserve good things, and I'm so glad that you've let me in to provide you with some of them. More to come, I hope.

It's hard to say these things...almost like I'll 'jinx' myself and a voice will tell me: ha ha only kidding! Don't worry, it's merely my mood this morning....I'm not nearly that cynical.....at the end of the day, I must be more optimistic than cynical because ... I choose to believe something really good is happening..... Yes, you should believe it, because so do I. The more we chat about our feelings, the easier it should be for us to express them fully and without hesitation. So far, you're doing great . . . and inspiring me to open up to you.

You are in my thoughts, Scott

On Mon, Nov 13, 2017 at 02:55 PM, Lisa wrote:

*When I read what you've written to me I think:
I am a fortunate woman ...... and I'm going to
embrace every happiness and stop questioning
EVERY thing as I usually do....* <u>Good for you.
I believe you'll be even happier if you do that.</u>

*The L word. I wrote about the capacity to love and
thought.... maybe I shouldn't even (dare) say that
word much less write it......* <u>Well . . . I think you may
be dancing a bit around telling me exactly how
you feel about "us", so I've decided to take the
lead on this one, like you did at the moment of our
first --- but hopefully not last --- wonderful kiss.

I'm not afraid any more to say that I love you,
Lisa. I love you because we seem to have a lot in
common and share many of the same ideas and
ideals. I love your independence because
I cherish mine, too. I love the fact that our not
being able to spend more time together makes me
very sad. I love that we both seem to feel our daily
messages have brought us closer together, even
though we're apart physically, and that continuing
our conversations will make us into even stronger
intellectual soulmates. And I love that I'm
attracted to you as a man should be attracted to a</u>

woman in a more-than-friends relationship. Your passionate kiss made me believe that you have similar feelings for me, too, especially since you took the lead, and I'm therefore hoping that the physical aspect of our relationship will also bloom if you agree that it should. But I probably won't know what, when, or how to do something about that, so you may have to take the lead in that direction, too. I'm just not very good at all at reading the signs.

So there it is, Lisa. I love you for who you are, for how you've treated me as someone very special, and for what we've done together.
I love you, at the very least, because I believe you're my soulmate . . . and later on, who knows? Maybe just that, which would be enough to sustain the loving feelings I have for you now, but perhaps more as we get to know each other even better. My hope *"springs eternal"*, as the writer Alexander Pope said, that in the not-too-distant future, you'll be able to say whether you feel the same loving way about me. And again, I'm so happy that you're feeling better.

But it makes the world go 'round. It's at the heart of everything magical and wonderful. It's the reason certain music moves us to tears . It's joyous and motivating and all things good......

I am so happy!!!!

On Tue, Nov 14, 2017 at 12:04 AM, Lisa wrote:

. . . *I love you too, Scott. I know this like I know my own name. There are so many reasons why....and I thank those lucky stars we found each other....*
So much to say. Will save most for when I see you.......it's late and need to sleep....and I want to dream about you....all night.....

Subject: Re: Some Close-to-Midnight Thoughts
Date: 11/15/17 at 02:30:35 PM, Scott wrote:

. . . I have some things to say which I've inserted into your text and underlined below. See you soon . . . but not soon enough.

On Wed, Nov 15, 2017 at 09:20 AM, Lisa wrote:

Dear Scott:
No one on God's green earth has ever quoted E.B.B. to me and evoked the passion I feel right now.........no one has sent me poetry or spoken so freely about love and everything it means like you have done. We agreed to be open and honest with each other, and that's all I'm doing. And I have passionate feelings as I'm doing that, just as you have when you receive my words. There is a special something you have, the ability to talk about your heart and not hold back.........it is your gift to me, and one I cherish and if the world ended today, it would remain close to my soul and sustain me......
I'm floating above the clouds. <u>Wow! No one has ever said something like that to me, Lisa. I'm getting misty again.</u>

<u>Since you seem to like the quotes I've been sending, here's another: "Absence makes the heart grow fonder", penned by a woman named Stickland in the 1800's. I agree, and so I hope that I can hold back the tears of joy when I see you tonight because I don't want to embarrass you . . . but I don't think I can make that hope a promise. I'll do my best.</u>

I woke up still feeling a bit 'off' but read your message and I believe I feel so much better. I know I do. I cannot wait to see you tonight and there is much I want to tell you. All good. All from MY heart.

You write about coincidences and connections and things that are fated to be. I'm thinking the universe may really work that way and always has. I wasn't always paying attention, and now I do. I'm thinking also that your wife was a wonderful person and knew you well and knew herself. I'd like to discuss all of this further with you sometime. <u>*The fact that you love to talk about things like that, as do I, is one of your most endearing qualities --- one of the many reasons that I've come to love you as I do.*</u>

Sometimes I feel the need to explain myself because, as my dear sister says, I tend to do things " ass.backward" and not think about consequences. When Joey came into my life, it was after years of living alone and I craved a relationship. He was above board about his own needs (which had nothing to do with a relationship) and he was, and still is, working on a website and since I write, I would help with content. A few times, we tried. (or I tried) to get closer, but it wasn't happening.

And I knew it never would. I feel I will always be friends with him, on some level, and know he has to move on. Yesterday, he suggested that (and this is in the middle of packing) he would have no trouble staying and I could live my own life ....and I said, NO!!!! NO and NO!!!

I miss my independence. And I found, that in spite of his tough facade, he is needier than I will ever be. He told me stories about his own childhood that would make Mary Poppins cringe. Awful. I guess what I want to tell you is, there is nothing, there has been nothing, intimate or romantic. <u>*Even if there was, Lisa, I hope you believe me when I say it wouldn't make any difference in how I feel about you.*</u>
Times I thought...hmm maybe...and I was met with less than kind responses. He has no 'filters' but now I know he did me a huge favor.

That is in the past now. I am optimistic, hopeful, and am discovering every day what real love is. I just hope I can be that person you believe in.

I am flawed ...we all are ..... but as time goes on and all my annoying bad habits are revealed to you, I hope you will continue to love me. <u>Although we really started learning about each other a relatively short time ago, I have no doubt that any of your qualities which could deliver a death blow to our relationship --- somewhat akin to the "fatal flaws" which were the ruination of characters in Shakespeare's tragedies --- would have revealed themselves to me by now. So as one of my favorite Beach Boys' songs says, "Don't worry, baby. Everything will turn out alright."</u>

I only have eyes for you, dear Scott.

Subject: Shakespeare's Definition of Love
Date: 11/20/17 at 09:55:05 AM, Scott wrote:

I've inserted Shakespeare's Sonnet 116 which I was trying to remember last night at the end of this email. In a nutshell, it means that true love --- the kind that I have for you --- will never wane no matter what. If someone's romantic feelings for another are, in fact, shattered or even diminished for any reason, then he or she was never truly in love in the first place. So don't worry about those flaws that you keep saying you have. It's too late for them --- real or imaginary --- to make any difference in my love for you. You're just stuck with my never-ending devotion, I'm afraid, but I hope you'll always believe that's a good thing.

SONNET 116

Let me not to the marriage of true minds
Admit impediments. Love is not love
Which alters when it alteration finds,
Or bends with the remover to remove:
O no; it is an ever-fixed mark,
That looks on tempests, and is never shaken;
It is the star to every wandering bark,
Whose worth's unknown, although his height be taken.
Love's not Time's fool, though rosy lips and cheeks
Within his bending sickle's compass come;
Love alters not with his brief hours and weeks,
But bears it out even to the edge of doom.
If this be error and upon me proved,
I never writ, nor no man ever loved.

On Mon, Nov 20, 2017 at 10:11 AM, Lisa wrote:

I believe you have convinced me that I am worthy of this love...through words and actions, the way you look at me, my ability to bare my soul to you so freely....and how you listen without judgement. There was a time before you came into my life but I hardly remember it...because now you are such a part of it. I love you.

Subject: What a Joy You Are !!
Date: 11/21/17 at 06:45:25 PM

When I got home today, I went to bed for my usual afternoon nap and woke up thinking about the wonderful experience I had watching you with the people at the Bohemia facility. Your warmth and affection toward them was awesome, as was their response to you in kind. Even if I didn't have the romantic love for you that I do, I would love you for the joy you brought into their world.

You're an amazing woman, Lisa, which I'm more aware of every time we're together. I haven't always done the right thing by my fellow human beings, but my giving you the chance to share your tenderness with those people today was undoubtedly one of the best things I've ever done. You've made me ". . . the happiest guy in the whole USA."

I hope to see you at McGill's tomorrow. In the meantime, I'll just express for the millionth time my boundless love for you. Thank you for being you . . . and for being with me.

On Tue, Nov 21, 2017 at 07:25 PM, Lisa wrote:

hi Scott:
Thank YOU for allowing me to share the day with you. I enjoyed every minute and the people were awesome! I was thinking before about how true it is that a minute, a second, can change the course of a life...how we are conceived how we grow how we move from the womb to be born...and how we can be oxygen deprived a little too long and be born into a life that wasn't expected.
It's a life nonetheless
It's a life deserving respect
Okay, I will stop philosophizing (sp?)
I had so much fun!
Jake's was fun as well
YOU are fun!
You are sweet and I love you!

On Mon, Nov 27, 2017 at 08:21 PM, Lisa wrote:

YOU are amazing. And I respond to you.
Can't wait until Wednesday, sweet Scotty!!!!!!

Subject: RE: I guess we covered everything in our phone conversation.......
Date: 11/27/17 at 10:28:13 PM

Everything that I do for you, and with you, and to you is because I love you, Lisa. I've tried to find words to adequately express my feelings, but they almost always seem to fall short.

Someone --- I'm not sure who --- once said, "The **best** feelings are those that have no words to describe them." If that's true, it's a shame, because I desperately want to find those words so that you'll know exactly why and how deeply I love you. I'll keep trying . . .

On Dec 3, 2017 at 10:50 PM, Scott wrote:

These last few days with you have been simply marvelous. I hope you feel the same way, despite my nutty and clumsy behavior today.

Attached is the picture of us at the Sunset Diner. It surely illustrates what gorgeous eyes and lovely smile you have, as I've been saying.
I nearly melt away each time I look at you.

On Dec 17, 2017 at 8:19 PM, Lisa wrote:

Will be fun to have you here again! So sorry I will be running back and forth ...it is what I do these days. Love ya, Scotty!!!!

Subject: Re: FW: looking ahead to Next Week
Date: 12/17/17 at 10:08:07 PM

It's going to be tough waiting until Wednesday to see you again, but at least I have fond memories --- and perhaps even dreams --- to keep me company until then. And I have Shakespeare's words, such as those below from his Sonnet 18. He often seems to have been writing just about you, reminding me of who and what you are to me.
I love you dearly, my darling.

Shall I compare thee to a summer's day?
Thou art more lovely and more temperate:
Rough winds do shake the darling buds of May,
And summer's lease hath all too short a date:
Sometime too hot the eye of heaven shines,
And often is his gold complexion dimm'd;
And every fair from fair sometime declines,
By chance, or nature's changing course, untrimm'd;
But thy eternal summer shall not fade
Nor lose possession of that fair thou ow'st;
Nor shall Death brag thou wander'st in his shade,

When in eternal lines to time thou grow'st;
So long as men can breathe or eyes can see,
So long lives this, and this gives life to thee.

On Jan 3, 2018 at 4:36 PM, Lisa wrote:

hi Scotty: Glad you are home...and even happier you will forego McGill's.....not because I begrudge you some fun, but because there's no telling what the weather will be. I will be snuggled under a blanket with Prince, reading or watching the tube. Of course, I will be thinking about you and what a great time we had.
You are a sweet, loving man and I am so happy we met each other. I know I said it already, but Happy New Year, Scotty!
I think 2018 will be amazing in many ways.
It already is.....

Subject: A Wednesday Night Love Note
Date: 01/03/18 at 09:02:51 PM, Scott wrote:

I did have a wonderful time with you during the past few days . . . lots of fun and still learning about you so that I can make you even happier than I hope I already have. Why? Because I love you, and doing things with and for you makes me very, very, VERY happy, too.

* * * * * * * * * * * * *

(Editor's Poetic Note)

As Lisa's and Scott's ship sets sail,
  will the rising trade winds of love prevail?
Or will theirs be just one more tale
  of devastating heartbreak, misery, and woe,
  like that of Juliet and her beloved Romeo
  and tragedies penned by the infamous Poe,
  as well as others of his ilk through the ages?
Want to find out? Keep turning these pages.

Chapter 3

Two Men in Lisa's Life

* * * * * * *

Subject: Please Read This Message --- Perhaps My Last Date: 01/23/18 at 11:42:59 PM

You may think that it's unfair for me to write this message to you after our last phone conversation, Lisa, but if you do love me, I ask that you read it. To avoid further heartbreak for both of us, though, I promise not to get in touch with you again unless you contact me first.

I think it's important for you to know that I now realize one of the worst things that can happen to a person --- and maybe the worst --- is for someone you deeply love to tell you that she never wants to see you again. The very idea that I'll never again be able to see you, to talk with you, to sing with you, to kiss you, to hold you in my arms, and to make love to you is so devastating right now that I can't fully comprehend nor even accept that reality yet.

I'm not telling you this to be mean --- I assume that you're hurting, too, and may even be more confused than I am --- but because I love you and don't want you to create a situation where someone else might experience what I did tonight. I believe that may very well happen again if during your "trial period" with Joey, one of you wants to stay together but the other one doesn't. I wish that I could be optimistic, say that probably won't happen, and wish you both well, but I'm sorry . . . I can't.

From my experience, a person's personality and behavior --- especially a man's --- doesn't usually change that much over the years, especially at our stage in life. Someone might feign changes or even give them a try in order to get what he or she wants, but from what I've seen, the person's true nature eventually surfaces again and can lead to devastating results. I hate to admit I did something like that several times during my younger years in my relationships with women, and I've seen other men do it, too, so I know that this sort of thing is all too real --- and quite common.

Joey had a year-and-a-half to treat you well and pursue a romantic relationship, but he didn't, so

I still have no idea at this point why you think that will change. In my opinion, the fact that he's willing to break us up by asking you to take him back with apparently no remorse nor compassion for the feelings of others --- especially me --- confirms that what I've just said above probably applies to him. I'm therefore begging you as a man who loves you dearly to give the matter much more thought --- and to discuss it with some friends, relatives, and maybe others whose wisdom and opinions you trust --- before making your final decision, since doing those things could save your life.

Unless I tell you differently, I'll stop by your place before going to McGill's Wednesday night sometime between 8:00 and 8:30 to pick up my things and leave your key on the kitchen table. I'll say something loud enough when I come in so that if you're home, you can go into one of the back rooms and won't have to see or talk with me, since you've indicated that's what you want. It does seem to be too unhappy an end to a relationship which I mistakenly thought was wonderful enough to be lasting. I hope that someday, I'll have a better understanding of why that wasn't so. I do wish you all the best.

On Wed, Jan 24, 2018 at 10:23 AM, Lisa wrote:

never never think you are less than terrific....I am the flawed one, I have a lifetime of things to work out. I doubt they will ever be resolved, so consider yourself lucky that you are out of this relationship... Find someone as nice as you are. I am sorry I caused you pain.

Subject: A Reply to Your Latest Email
Date: 01/24/18 at 01:48:27 PM

Since you wrote to me, I feel that I'm allowed to reply.

To me, your saying "I am the flawed one" is akin to what's said in many movies when one person breaks up with another --- that is, *"It's not you, it's me."* What that generally means, though, is that the person speaking wants to break up for other reasons and doesn't want the other party to know what they are but instead is merely trying to soften the blow.

Following that up with "*I have a lifetime of things to work out. I doubt they will ever be resolved, so consider yourself lucky that you are out of this relationship*" doesn't help either because I've said on a number of occasions that I'd be there to help you through anything, <u>which is without a doubt preferable to losing you</u>. But instead of allowing me to continue doing that, you're permitting what I thought was a relationship based on mutual love and support through thick and thin to be destroyed in favor of going back to a man who, by your own admission, rejected your efforts to build that kind of relationship with you, didn't treat you very well, and never even told you that he loves you. Common sense indicates that will only add to your problems, not help to resolve them, making me think the things that you said are just more excuses for breaking up with me.

You've made me believe the things I did for and with you were insignificant, since you're willing to accept Joey back with open arms instead of my being worth keeping around. I feel that I did my best, and if my best wasn't good enough, perhaps I'm not meant to be in any kind of relationship.

My final words are that I feel I did find someone as nice as me --- YOU. But you've already said that you won't even let me discuss this matter further with you and try to win you back, and that's what hurts the most, making me think that you hold me in very low esteem and that perhaps you don't love me nearly as much as I thought. Please let me know if you ever change your mind about that because I'm finding it impossible to understand and cope with this situation, and without further clarification from you, I'm not sure that I ever will. If you don't love me enough to help me with that, I may just try to avoid people as much as I can to minimize the chance of further heartbreaks because right now, I'm totally dazed and confused and don't know how to deal with this.

On Wed, Jan 24, 2018 at 02:56 PM, Lisa wrote:

I do not hold you in low esteem. There may be truth to other things, but that is NOT TRUE.
I elevated you and I know I am not on your level. I doubt I could ever be....
Leading to; please stay open and trust people!!! if I have ruined your ability to trust, I am worse than I thought
I don't know how to explain. I understand that saying.....I'm the flawed one...sounds like a load. Maybe I didn't see that. Maybe you are right. I think I have a personality disorder. But that is another story.

I tried and tried to forget Joey. I put him out of my mind whenever he popped in. But he crept into dreams, and I knew suddenly that I needed to resolve this. He said all the things I had waited to hear. Is he truthful? I don't know. It could be a disaster. It could work but it could fall apart. 50/50. That it all crashed down on you is something I will never forgive myself for.

I don't think I have done such a horrible thing in my lifetime...and if I ever do again, I would rather leave the planet, die, disappear, than hurt someone in this way. You trusted me, you loved me. And I repaid you this way..........like a low disgusting inhuman being. I know you think this and of course...that is what I am. I will own this and probably regret it.
I've only heard about this, people who have this uncanny hold on other people. He has that kind of hold on me. I have to find out if he has any feelings to back it.

I will always love you, Scotty. I am sorry to be such a disappointment to you and I am sorry you want me completely out of your life, but I cannot fault you for that.

Subject: A Plea for Help
Date: 01/24/18 at 04:59:32 PM

That's the thing, Lisa. I DON'T want you completely out of my life. I want you in it, and that's the problem. You now have, as you put it, that "uncanny hold" on me. I can't get you out of my mind --- nor my heart. You've given my life new meaning, and without that, I don't know what will become of me. As things stand now, I truly believe that everything else will become pointless and insignificant if I should lose you.
I therefore desperately want to understand why you're so willing to give up what he have, and could continue to have for a long time, for what appears to me to be just the same pipe dream that you've already tried without success to turn into something real.

I know that you said discussing this situation wouldn't be helpful, but if you don't think it would help you, I definite believe it might help me to understand and cope because our emails haven't been doing the job. So if you do love me as you say, and if you want to help me avoid having what's left of my life come crashing down along with my sanity if you leave me in the dark, I implore you to sit down and talk with me to try to clarify what's going on and why. I hope that we can do that tonight when I come by around 8:00 to pick up my things. I'm pleading with you to let me do that at least for my sake . . . and perhaps for yours, too. You can let me know one way or the other when I get there.

Subject: I'm Home . . . and Thanks
Date: 01/25/18 at 01:39:16 AM

As promised, I'm letting you know that I arrived home safe and sound --- later than expected, though, because there were only a handful of singers at McGill's, so I decided to stay almost until closing and sang 6 or 7 tunes. I could have used your help because there was a lady there who wouldn't leave me alone in spite of Sharon's and Dotty's efforts to help me and my telling her that I have a girlfriend.

Thanks again for allowing me to discuss our relationship, etc. with you at such length tonight. You were able to clarify many issues and gave me hope that there's a chance we can be together again someday. Nothing would make me happier because I love you so much.

On Thu, Jan 25, 2018 at 07:32 AM, Lisa wrote:

I'm so happy we talked. I'm so happy you don't think I'm a monster. you are an amazing person!!!

thank you for letting me know you got home safe....

Subject: An Idea Which I Hope You'll Like, Too
Date: 01/25/18 at 10:14:57 PM

An idea came to me when I was showering a little while ago that I'm extremely excited about and therefore want to share with you in this message. I hope that you'll be as thrilled with it as I am.

You may recall that I wrote the following In one of the emails I sent to you after you told me about Joey coming back.

> "I think it's important for you to know that I now realize one of the worst things that can happen to a person --- and maybe the worst --- is for someone you deeply love to tell you that she never wants to see you again. The very idea that I'll never again be able to see you, to talk to you, to sing with you, to kiss you, to hold you in my arms, and to make love to you is so devastating right now that I can't fully comprehend nor even accept that reality yet."

I still feel the same way --- and maybe even more so --- because although I sincerely appreciate your agreeing to the ideas we discussed last night in order to stay in each other's lives, they can't possibly come close to giving us everything we once had together. You also asked me whether I thought it was possible for you to love two men, to which I said "yes" because you're living proof of that.

With those things in mind, I can't think of any reason why you couldn't have the best of both worlds by allowing the two men who love you to have a simultaneous relationship with you to the fullest extent possible. I feel that would be more beneficial and fair to all three of us than your having to choose between Joey and me, and cutting me out of your life almost completely in the meantime. Here's how that could work.

Joey will be living with you, at least for now, so you should have plenty of time with him during the "trial period" to determine if he has indeed made the drastic and hopefully permanent changes in his life which he promised so that he can be a meaningful part of yours. However, unless I somehow misjudged <u>our</u> situation, I feel that all aspects of the relationship we enjoyed were extremely beneficial to both of us and have given our lives new meaning and purpose, which could become even better if we would resume where we left off by your staying with me from time to time --- e.g., perhaps two or three days and nights every two or three weeks while Joey takes care of your place and Prince. That would enable us to still reap all of the benefits from the wonderful type of relationship we had which, in my opinion, would be a crime to lose, even temporarily.

I think it's important for you to know that I was jealous of Joey before only because I thought you'd have to choose between the two of us if you let him back into your life. However, I've given this matter a lot of thought, and I can promise you that I wouldn't be jealous at all if you decided to have relationships with both of us. I also think it would be a true test of Joey's promise to put you first by your asking him to agree to this scenario.

You'd obviously benefit because you'd still be with the two men you love to the fullest extent possible without having to choose between us. I also believe it's quite likely that Joey hasn't or perhaps can't change everything that you're hoping he did but has qualities which would make a continuing relationship of some sort with him worthwhile for you. That would seem to be most possible if you continued your relationship with me so that I can help fill in the gaps left in your life . . . and in mine, which right now are enormous because of where I stand.

Both Joey and I would benefit in many other ways, too. For example, I believe it would be much more stressful --- and maybe even impossible --- for either one of us to give you everything you need from a man, but by your having relationships with both of us, Joey and I would only have to concentrate on your needs which each of us separately is in the best position to satisfy.

I'm really excited about this plan, Lisa, which I honestly believe is the fairest and most beneficial way to try to satisfy the needs that you, Joey, and I have based on our love for each other . . . and to make all of us very happy in the end. Therefore, after reading this message several times and perhaps discussing it with other folks, I dearly hope that you'll agree to give it a try right away for all of our sakes. In the meantime, please let me know if you have any initial questions or observations by email, or by phone if you think that would be better.

On Fri, Jan 26, 2018 at 09:05 AM, Lisa wrote:

I have to admit that the content of your email was a surprise to me. I never thought you would consider something like this.....and I'm not sure why....but it is something I've thought about.

Is there selfishness on my part? Probably so. I've never wanted to walk away from you, you are special to me. I don't think I can get over the fact that you still want me in your life.

*I would ask you to give me a little time to think it over. This is because I'm impulsive and need to consider my choices more carefully than I do.
I have never been in this position before and never thought I would be. Yes. I love you both dearly, but differently. I think you understand this.*

Dear Scotty....special...is an understatement. it barely scratches the surface of who you are.....

Subject: Thanks for Your Initial Thoughts About My Proposal
Date: 01/26/18 at 11:57:28 AM

I'm so glad that you've already thought about something like the plan I've proposed. Maybe it is selfish on your part --- and mine, too --- but I think we both would agree that selfishness is definitely preferable to losing the wonderful relationship we have. I can live with selfishness, but without you, my life will be empty, and without me, I have no doubt that your life will be far from complete, too, regardless of how things work out with Joey.

Neither of us should have to live with that, so take your time, but please know in the meantime I meant every word in my email. In fact, Joey's coming back may be a blessing in disguise. Why do I say that? Because if you agree with the plan I've proposed, I firmly believe that not only can you take care of the "unfinished business" which would otherwise be on your mind for the rest of your life, but also that by doing so and keeping me in your life at the same time, you and I can continue to share the love and good times which have made us so happy and our lives so much more meaningful than they were before we got together.

It may even be better for us than before because you're taking steps to lift the cloud that's been hanging over you, which undoubtedly has had a negative impact on our relationship, as long as you don't replace it with another cloud by cutting me out of your life. The more I reflect on what I've proposed, the more I believe all of this was meant to be, and that the plan I've outlined provides a perfect solution to make our love and lives much more complete than they otherwise would be by getting rid of the sorrow and hollowness which all of us are currently feeling to one degree or another.

As I previously said, you should take your time to consider this matter carefully because the happiness and fulfilled lives of three people are at stake. I only hope that it won't take too long to get back to me again --- and to hopefully let me back into your life --- because my loving heart will keep breaking in the meantime.

Subject: my last email......
Date: 01/27/18 at 02:45:13 PM

... I have a lot to discuss with you and hope maybe we can talk via phone soon ....or meet Weds at McGill's and talk a bit then.

Don't know where to start. Maybe with this: I do love you and I don't want to lose that love. You are dear to me, even though you must be thinking I've lost my mind. Never in my life did
I think I would be contemplating a relationship with two people.....but sometimes it makes sense...and sometimes a wee puritanical voice screams: don't do it! But I drown that voice out. I am only interested in being happy, in helping you find happiness......and then there's Joey.....

You must wonder about him. Complicated...that is an understatement. We talked this morning and I know this: he gets it. No one really knows how it will progress, whether it will work....I say, throw caution to the wind. Caution is overrated anyway. I told him you are important to me in so many ways. He doesn't want to be regarded as a fool but his interests in this stage of his life are not with physical love .... something I didn't understand....and now I do. It's not a case of...

*he doesn't love me. I really think he does. And
I know you do as well. You both are so different,
and so is your love.*

*I hope you understand what I just wrote.
Confusing? yes. Impossible? no no no. I want you
both in my life!!! Don't know if it will work for all
if us....but hoping it does.*

*And p.s....I miss you. If you can accept my
weirdness and quirks, you are amazing..but I knew
that already....*

*I am anxious to hear from you, to hear what you
think. please, please, don't let old school rules or
sensibilities get in the way. I know this could be
right. I know how I feel.*

Subject: Re: . . . Saturday Plans
Date: 01/27/18 at 04:07:56 PM

I'm here, dearest Lisa, and very anxious to talk with
you, too. I would prefer to do that face-to-face
rather than by phone if that's okay with you.

What if we got together for dinner somewhere
(e.g., at the SD?), even as early as Sunday night?
That would be a more peaceful environment than a

karaoke session and therefore would enable us to think and talk much better. Please let me know. And if you get home early enough tonight, perhaps you could stop by The Oasis for a bit so that we could start talking there as best that we can and have a little fun, too.

I would like to say more in this email, but I have to get ready for Church now. Just one thought before I sign off. I believe it would be very helpful when we do discuss this situation --- perhaps with some thoughts from you in an email beforehand --- for you to explain, as best you can, the specific differences between the love you have for me and for Joey, and what benefits you and your two men should expect to reap if both of us had a continuing relationship with you. With that as a starting point, I believe that we can develop the plans needed to make all three of us happy and have much more. Just remember how strong my love for you is.

On Jan 29, 2018 at 9:32 AM, Scott wrote:

After we spoke, I decided that it might be best to forget about your staying over Tuesday night or your coming here on Wednesday morning.

I would have liked that support and extra time with you, but I shuttered when you said "*maybe this thing isn't doable after all*", indicating to me that you might be ready to cut me out of your life for good. I guess I put too much pressure on you, but after all we've done to stay together in our wonderful relationship, the fact that you'd even consider that again made the blood rush out of my head. I don't want my life --- and maybe yours, too --- to come crashing down in flames for any reason . . . I'm scared to death again now . . .

Subject: Re: Let's Reconsider My Last Email
Date: 01/29/18 at 09:43:06 AM, **Lisa** wrote:

pls don't doubt me!

I chgd weds appt and I will meet you in the morning. I know it's important to you....and to me too

will talk more later. don't jump to conclusions....I love you!!!!

I just need a little breathing room.....I need some time to move furniture around and rearrange my place..

it is topsy turvy and, believe it or not, I do need some semblance of order, lol

Subject: Only Misunderstandings, Not Mistrust
Date: 01/29/18 at 04:53:49 PM, Scott wrote:

I got your phone message, and in view of its content and length, I agree that we should have a serious chat again tonight. Anytime after 8 p.m. would be good for me. Before we do, though, I want to clarify a few things.

First of all, I hope you'll believe me when I say there's never, NEVER been an undercurrent of mistrust on my part with respect to anything you've said or done. Sometimes I wished you had given me more advanced notice, especially about Joey's returning, but I've never doubted anything you've told me and don't anticipate that I ever will.

Secondly, I know that on a few occasions, my initial reactions to something you've said may have led you to believe I've felt that you haven't been honest with me. Those situations arose, I believe, only because of the way you said them and, perhaps more importantly, the order in which things were said. I'd like to use Joey's sleeping arrangements as a prime example of what I mean.

I assumed that when he was living in your place before, he had his own bed in the little room, and you later verified that. You also said that he wasn't interested in a physical relationship, and that you now understood that. Then at dinner, I asked just out of curiosity how you could get his bed into that room because there didn't seem to me to be a space for it. You responded just by saying that he's sleeping in your bed without first clarifying why that was --- i.e., because you sold the bed after he left and you therefore had no alternative when he moved back in, but that it was like sleeping with your brother and that no sex nor romance was anticipated on either of your parts.

Without previously hearing the reasons, my imagination ran wild. That was my bad because I've always trusted you and believed what you've told me about everything. It also hit me hard because one of the things that I wanted to chat with you about, which we later did at the S.D., was if I could resume staying over at your place in order to maximize our time together and to enable you to take care of your other personal business which you couldn't do as easily if you only stayed over in my condo. But after you said Joey's sleeping in your bed, I quickly assumed that staying overnight in your apartment would never be possible, thus greatly limiting our time together. Therefore, if you had said something like the following when I asked the question about bed placement in Joey's room, I honestly believe that the incident would have had a completely different outcome.

    "Well, Scotty, I sold Joey's bed after he moved out, so I've been letting him sleep in my bed because we currently have no choice. But there's no sex involved because as I've said before, Joey isn't interested in that, and on my part, it's like sleeping with my brother."

That's why, Lisa, I like to communicate by email whenever possible. That gives me enough time to think about the words and their order so I can avoid misinterpretations and misunderstandings as much as possible. But because of your phone message, I'm thinking that I must have said something in my last email to make you bring up the subject of mistrust when I was just trying to clarify the details of our get togethers this week and put forth a few more options for you to consider. If you felt otherwise, or for whatever other reasons you're wondering if I'm not trusting you, please let me know when we talk this evening so that I can avoid doing that again and adding to the stress which you're obviously feeling. I only want all of us to be happy and in appropriate relationships with each other, so hopefully the above and our chat later on will let us keep going toward that goal.

Subject: I'm Feeling Great This Morning Despite the Snow !!
Date: 01/30/18 at 10:58:33 AM

. . . I'm sooooo happy this morning that our most recent emails and phone conversations have had such positive outcomes. I really think that we're all on the right track now, and I can't find words to adequately express my joy and appreciation because you and Joey are going to such lengths to enable me to resume my visits to you. I never had any doubts about your love for me, but your efforts to resolve the sleeping arrangements issue, which would have greatly limited our time together if you left it the way it was, leads me to believe that your love for me is even stronger and deeper than I imagined. To paraphrase the Donna Fargo tune, that makes me ". . . the happiest guy in the whole USA."

On Sat, Feb 03, 2018 at 10:41 AM, Lisa wrote:

I was just thinking about the blessings in my life, beginning with you. You are the most caring and loving person, and not afraid to show your feelings!! Joey is floundering a bit and unsure, but he is getting used to things I think. My kids: well, a bit stormy, but they will get used to me too. I am different and the same...just more vocal about my life and needs.

will meet you at The Oasis tonight...8? that is fine.....and looking forward to a lazy relaxing morning with you. Life is good. as long as you are in mine. You are a sweet, sexy, amazing man!!!

Subject: Re: Great News for Both of Us
Date: 02/03/18 at 12:09:29 PM, Scott wrote:

Your last email isn't the longest, but it's probably the best one that I've ever received from you. What wonderful things you said about me, especially that the blessings in your life begin with me !! I'm getting teary with happiness.

I'm so looking forward to seeing you again at The Oasis. And yes, 8:00 would be fine to give us time to talk a bit before we sing . . . I can hardly wait to see you again, my love. I adore you.

On Feb 4, 2018 at 8:56 PM, Lisa wrote:

*I was going to call and decided to write instead...this was our #1 mode of communication initially, and I am feeling sentimental tonight....
I was in front of computer before, headphones on.....listening to the music that means something to me.....music that evokes feelings....the background of my whole life. Does everyone feel this way about music? I doubt it,
I doubt thin-skinned folks could stand the emotions that some music unleashes..*

*An old familiar (to me) song made me cry....for many reasons. It was a song I played over and over after my husband passed.... it said what
I was thinking......it gave me hope that I'd see him again. And it's simply a wonderful song. When I heard it before, my thoughts were elsewhere. I saw a movie, in my mind, of everything that transpired last night...of you.......of me........of a winter sky.....a crowded bar........a warm bed.
It made me cry.
But happy. This time. Everything's good*

On Mon, Feb 12, 2018 at 07:59 PM, Lisa wrote:

I have no doubt that I love you...and need you...in a way that surprises even myself.
I didn't realize it could be intense at this stage
of life, that we need things we always
needed! And, dadgumit, we deserve to be happy!
PS. I am
(I got you, babe)
Yours with a smile...

Subject: You're So Right About Us
Date: 02/12/18 at 10:33:33 PM

All of what you said is true, sweet Lisa. I've actually known those things almost since the time we admitted we were in love with each other. I've known that I need you, and that you also need me, to be happy. It's just taken you a bit longer to fully grasp that because you were hoping for more love and devotion from Joey than he can offer, for whatever reason. But lately, the things you've said to me --- and especially the way you've said them --- have made me truly believe that you now realize how futile it would be to keep trying to find what you want and need in any other direction than the one that leads straight to me. And does that make me happy? You're so right if you answered "yes".

Sweet dreams, my love.

On Tue, Feb 13, 2018 at 09:46 AM, Lisa wrote:

Joey is sleeping in his own room, hurray hurray.......and I enjoyed my own space, my own bed. ahhh. It finally got thru to him that I was uncomfortable and he needed to step it up . . .

There is a Proust quote, something about love's 'charming gardener' causing it to blossom and grow. You are my charming gardener....

ttyl...love you so much

Subject: What Nice Surprises
Date: 02/13/18 at 10:37:52 AM

Oh, my!! What great news about you finally reclaiming your room, sweet Lisa, and what a nice thought about my being your gardener.
Of course, even the best gardener can't make a woman's love "blossom and grow" unless she has a beautiful heart and soul to begin with and he treats her with tender loving care. That's been our reality all along, so I'm not at all surprised by the outcome . . . 'Til we chat again, remember that you're the one and only woman in my life, and

how thankful I am for that. As I've said many times before, I'm a very lucky man.

Subject: You're On My Mind . . .
Date: 02/14/18 at 05:19:50 AM

Hi Lisa, my love ~ Went to bed about midnight, only slept 'til 2:00 --- thinking of you. Now it's 5:00, and you're still in my thoughts, and in my heart. I guess I'm just hopelessly in love with you. Neptune's swimming all around his tank, so maybe he's longing to see you, oo. Stomach's rumbling, so I ate some Girl Scout cookies. Delicious. Groggy --- going to try sleeping again. Am I crazy? No . . . only crazy in love with the perfect woman for me. Bye for now ---

On Thu, Feb 15, 2018 at 09:57 AM, Lisa wrote:

Oh Scotty...I am so sorry you didn't sleep well....as for your belief that you treated me badly ... well .... it is impossible and put that out of your mind! You treat me like a queen, all the time, every time I see you. You are so sensitive, another reason I love you so much....just because I was overtired, it's not your fault and being disappointed is ok. I love you, Scotty dear....
I know you wouldn't hurt me.....you are amazing!

More later....

On Sun, Mar 04, 2018 at 10:45 PM, Lisa wrote:

Hi Scotty:
Enjoying the Oscars...
Missing you.
Was a wonderful visit and I am hoping I dream about you tonight.........
I'm glad you are home and safe.....
Will write tomorrow.

Found a quote from Charles Schultz:
'All you need is love.
But a little chocolate now and then doesn't hurt.'

ok. cute. but what I really want to say is:
'I will carry you with me
til I see you again'
I love you my Scotty.........today...tomorrow forever.

On Tue, Mar 06, 2018 at 07:26 PM, Lisa wrote:

. . . It looks like this storm is downgraded, at least for the south shore. I so hope it's nothing big. The stores were crowded at 10 am today.....I just want everyone to be home and safe tomorrow .....IF it's big.

I have been working with Joey, going through the remaining boxes and stuffing as much as possible into the closet. Tomorrow I think we will put the bed together. Time to quit for today, and have dinner.
Had some interesting conversations. Will tell you Thursday. AND I miss you very much...(VERY).....thinking about how lucky we are!!! I love you, my dear.... how could I not love you, it is so easy!!!!!!!

On Mar 6, 2018 at 8:28 PM, Scott wrote:

I can always count on you, my dearest Lisa, to send me a great message. And as far as telling you where I'm going if you're not with me, I want to do that so you won't worry if I don't get back to you while I'm out. I'll also send you a goodnight message when I'm home again because I know that you worry whenever I go to a tavern alone.

Good luck with the bed tomorrow . . . and I'm dying to hear about those "interesting conversations".

It's easy to love you, too, but it hasn't always been easy to deal with situations that have come up in your life. However, I believe my love for you has grown because of our willingness to work together so tirelessly to overcome every obstacle to our relationship that has gotten in our way. And that's very comforting . . .

On Mar 11, 2018 at 3:28 PM, Scott wrote:

I'm thrilled that we were able to spend so much time together during my last visit. You're a remarkable women, and it's a pleasure and an honor to be with you.

I hope you're enjoying the parade and dinner with Sharon later. Call me after 8 p.m. if you'd like to. It would be wonderful to hear your voice, since I'm missing you already --- the only woman I'm in love with.

On Sun, Mar 11, 2018 at 06:09 PM, Lisa wrote:

I miss you too!
I don't think I need to say that....because from the time you drive away, to the next visit, I think about you....I think about how much fun we have together....
I think about your kind and considerate nature....I think about our talks, our laughs, and the sweetness and passion we share at night.
You have my heart.
You have me, heart and soul....

On Mon, Mar 12, 2018 at 08:39 PM, Lisa wrote:

I did read those ideas about 'love' 'in love' and they are fairly consistent......and, from what it says, I must be 'in love' with you, as well as loving you....but I doubt it matters. I know what I feel, and it's absolutely real....
However. I have felt an 'in love' feeling fleetingly at times....when I see something so absolutely amazing and precious, I have felt 'in love' for the moment. When I saw the squirrel begging this morning, I think I was 'in love' with the whole scene. Maybe that sounds silly, but
I could mean something else entirely. I don't even know. What I DO know is, I love you dearly.

I found a piece by Anne Sexton. I am not familiar with her work and want to read more. But here goes:

Love?
Be it man. Be it woman. It must be a wave you want to glide in on, give your body to it, give your laugh to it, give,, when the gravelly sand takes you, your tears to the land. To love another is something like prayer and can't be planned, you just fall into its arms because your belief undoes your disbelief.

I no longer feel the disbelief....maybe I feel relief. Relief that I can say out loud how much I love and respect you....Yes, relief and belief....that I love and that
I am loved back.

If it gets better, I cannot wait.
See you in my dreams tonight...

Subject: My Mistake --- but Now My Joy
Date: 03/12/18 at 11:01:20 PM

When you asked me tonight if I had read your email, and I said that I did, I was referring to one

I thought you had sent to me earlier today, but that was our first phone conversation. And so I just read your message below for the first time a short while ago and began to get misty.

To find a woman who feels the same way about me as I feel about her -- YOU -- is amazing and as close to a miracle as I've ever experienced. I don't care if it was God, angels, the alignment of planets and stars, or perhaps just a random set of circumstances making it happen because our relationship is so perfect that the reason it came to be doesn't matter to me. The only thing that matters is that "we" did happen, which turned out to be so very, very special for both of us. Anne Sexton might have observed that belief truly undid disbelief as we fell into love's outstretched arms.

I hope that other folks will continue to bask in the warmth of our love for years to come in this life and into the next. Now I'm really getting misty, so I better just wish you sweet dreams and sign off for tonight.

On Thu, Mar 29, 2018 at 11:02 AM, Lisa wrote:

Not a day goes by that I don't thank the heavens for how lucky, how fortunate I am. This is because you are in my life...you have changed my life...in such wonderful ways. And I thank you for sticking with me through the good, the bad, and the crazy. I know there are great things to come.......

*I love you very much my dear man . . .
see you later, can't hardly wait!!!!*

Subject: Re: Weekend Plans
Date: 03/29/18 at 11:37:29 AM

What a terrific way to start my day, my sweet Miss L --- with a wonderful email from my best friend and lover. I'm so anxious to see you, but we'll have to wait a few hours. I still have some chores to do here, and then I plan to take a nap and make stops for dinner and maybe at Jake's on the way, since I know it's on the bottom of your fun list. And as for great things to come . . . absolutely, because we already started that ball rolling months ago when we fell in love, which was, of course, the greatest thing of all !!!!!!!!

On Tue, Apr 03, 2018 at 10:05 PM, Lisa wrote:

hello my baby....yes, I miss you. I am curled up on couch with Prince. He is my shadow these days. I am tired, but don't want to sleep just yet....would rather picture your face in my mind....

what a great face, by the way! it's a book I love to read...it is a kind face, a happy face that laughs often and hard...a sweet face. that face makes me smile whenever I see it. I love your face... and I love you!

Chapter 4

Navigating Through More Rough Waters

* * * * * * *

On Apr 29, 2018 at 3:33 AM, Scott wrote:

Having strange thoughts and want to share them with you, even though they're not as positive as I'd like. For example . . . Is our relationship still growing, or is it heading south a bit? You seem to have lost some interest in our going to venues together as much these days, and your emails lately haven't included the hearts that I love to see. Does your wrapping yourself in the red comforter instead of getting under the blue one with me mean anything, such as you don't want to get close to me when you do that?

Does the same go for Prince? I know he's used to cuddling with you, but is your love for him so great that he has to come between us when I'm visiting and in bed with you? That certainly makes me feel second-class and puts a damper on our making love, but perhaps that's not as important to you as it is to me --- i.e., to show you how much I love you and make everything else we do together more meaningful --- especially since you use the term "fooling around" instead of "making love". I don't consider what we do fooling around, but if you do, maybe it indicates a difference in how we view that aspect of our relationship.

And is your missing Joey so much an indication that your "business" with him isn't finished after all? I was hoping that all the good things we have together would be strong enough to replace your feelings for a man who, as interesting to you as he might be --- the reasons for which are still a mystery to me --- treated you so badly with little or no remorse.

Sorry about my rambling, but we agreed to be honest with each other. I love you and always will, and I believe you love me, too, but it appears love isn't enough to overcome doubts in your mind about whether our relationship is as solid as I'd like to think, especially when you imagine things about me which I've never given you any reason to believe might be true.

I hope you can shed some light on the reasons that I'm feeling so insecure tonight because I'm at a loss to explain it. Perhaps a face-to-face discussion would help if I promise to try not to dwell excessively on what we say, since you seem to feel that's an annoying trait I have. In my defense, I only do that because I want to make sure any issues we have are fully resolved beyond any doubt so that we can have the type of lasting relationship I feel we both need and deserve.

On Sun, Apr 29, 2018 at 09:33 AM, Lisa wrote:

*Scotty my dear . . . I have been somewhat clueless about a few things, but now
I understand a bit more.*

Other than being long distance friends with Joey, there is no other business unfinished, no other feelings unsettled. I am positive about that. I tried hypothetically putting myself in your position and I know I would feel similarly, maybe even react with some anger. We are human and I get it. I hope it is not something that will be between us always. He doesn't deserve to be elevated to that and to ruin what we have. Did I miss him? yes. but I do not want him back.

*It is odd that I have had similar feelings this week, that something is 'off' and needs fixing. All of a sudden, you were busy and you disappeared in a way. No phone calls 'just to hear my voice' and I felt like...out of sight..etc.
I know you were busy, but I cried because you seemed to forget me. When that happens,
I eventually erect a brick wall.*

Your communications ceased to be flowery and warm. Read them. They are businesslike. It concerned me... lots.

I always wrap myself in that red blanket by the way. Nothing to do with you or how I feel about you. It is my Linus blanket. My safety blanket. It doesn't mean I wouldn't rather cuddle with YOU!

Prince. I know he takes up a lot of time and energy but deep down I am that crazy dog person. He is my comfort when things aren't right. He isn't 'just a dog' ...he is my little buddy....I would have a farm with dozens of dogs ....in my dreams. it won't happen in reality.

I will be more sensitive about that. I know he can be very annoying!

Going to karaoke is fun. But sometimes I want to do something else . . . Maybe, as time goes on, you are learning...perhaps WE are learning about each other's flaws and idiosyncrasies....seeing reality thru the veil of love and wondering how accepting we are! I think this is natural, but it's up to us to keep magic and excitement in the relationship. I thrive on magic. Without it, life is a series of events, time passing. We are advanced in age...we both have a lifetime of experiences ...we have baggage.

But I'm counting on the love, the magic, to define us. Not the baggage. We saw something in each other that was unique and now I'm realizing that yes, we need to talk face to face.......!

But for now, I will send this and wait for a reply. If you don't know by now, I love you very much!!! Maybe it's a good thing that we are thinking about how to proceed.....about what is happening...

*I want to make things better.
You are my sunshine.*

Subject: The Type of Message From You I Was Hoping For
Date: 04/29/18 at 11:44:30 AM

My sweet, sweet, sweet, sweet Lisa ~ I can't respond to everything you said now, but I was so relieved after reading your words. I was afraid that you might have wanted us to part company if I was as honest as I was, but instead, you wrote about reasons why we should stay together . . . and that's what I needed to hear, because I still feel we belong to each other in a very, very, VERY special way. Just the fact that you took the time to write so much about the way you feel about us says it all.

I'll call you this evening, probably after 8:00, so that we can talk further. In the meantime, please know that I believe more than ever that we can resolve any issue that comes up so that nothing --- ABSOLUTELY NOTHING --- will derail our love train.

Subject: Yesterday and Today
Date: 04/30/18 at 08:33:49 AM

I'm overjoyed with your messages and the phone conversation we had yesterday. I'm now convinced beyond the shadow of a doubt that our loving relationship will continue to blossom and remain healthy as long as we clear the air and shake off a little "baggage" from time to time. As I've said many times, I love you, need you, and want you in my life as long as you'll let me stay in yours, and since you said that you feel the same way, I see no reason in the world why we can't walk hand in hand down that path for many years to come . . .

After our discussion yesterday, I hope you realize even more than before that you're my one and only love, and if so, that makes me the happiest guy --- and I suspect it makes you the happiest gal --- in the whole U.S.A.

On Mon, Apr 30, 2018 at 11:33 AM, Lisa wrote:

Just reading about how happy you feel, combined with my own happiness, is a double shot of good feelings .. I am invigorated by our love and feelin' good.
You are my sunshine, always . . .

On Monday, May 14, 2018, Scott wrote:

Hello, dear Lisa ~   I'm home and finally settled back in, lonely and sad --- lonely because I'm not with you, and sad because of how we parted earlier.

I'm sure I mentioned to you after Beth called that I'd probably go home today and explained why I thought that would be best for both of us, especially since you were feeling so much better. Apparently, though, I didn't do a good job because you said as I was heading toward the door that you were surprised I was leaving today and looked both sad and mad. I'm going to try not to dwell on how that made me feel like a "bad boy" because my tendency to "overthink" bothers you, but I can't seem to get over issues in a New York minute like you do no matter how hard I try. I envy your ability to do that, but it's obviously much harder for me than for you. Anyway, I hope to talk with you tomorrow by email and/or phone, and I wish sweet dreams for you tonight.

On Tue, May 15, 2018 at 03:47 AM, Lisa wrote:

Up most of the night...
feeling so.so and sad after reading your note
..I am so SORRY I caused you to feel that way
...I guess I have ideas that are ridiculous...esp when
I don't feel well.....right now just restless, can't sleep
Will talk tomorrow when my head is clearer
Just a point: I don't get over things so quickly
...I just choose not to make a big deal about
them. My heart is burdened with so much
I think it will burst sometimes.....Love you much and
miss you

Subject: Please Let Me Help
Date: 05/15/18 at 08:47:00 AM

Even before I opened your email, I saw that you wrote it at around 4 a.m., so I suspected that you didn't sleep well. I hope that you get some rest today.

I had a feeling you don't get over things quickly, despite your facial and verbal expressions to the contrary. Everyone handles issues in different ways, but I believe that keeping them bottled up inside of you instead of resolving them when they come up isn't a positive thing for your emotional well-being. That burden may indeed cause you to burst some day and, in the meantime, lead you to say and do things that you wouldn't otherwise.

For example, we're always a little sad when I have to leave you, but we both know that's necessary to retain our independence and for me to get things done that I can only do at my place. I therefore don't want to feel as unhappy and guilty about going as I did yesterday because that makes leaving even harder. Just remember that I'm always available by phone, email, or face-to-face to listen so that you can vent your frustrations as they come up rather than letting them influence unrelated things because you keep them bottled up inside.

With that being said, I hope you'll use me as a sounding board more often than you have in the past so that both of us can be as happy and stress-free as possible.

On Tue, May 15, 2018 at 09:40 AM, Lisa wrote:

. . . is hard to explain why I act this way...I may have preconceived notions of how relationships should go...

I probably felt worse than I described to you....how could you know then!? You couldn't. So all I wanted was you to be there, maybe just holding me. I felt abandoned.

This being said, I also value my independence. I guess I want my cake etc etc. In fact, I don't know what the heck I want. I like my alone time, I want my Scott time.. all of it. I want to be honest with you, but I am afraid you will head for the hills if I tell you what I'm thinking.

I am going to be out later . . . don't know what time coming home. Will try to call you.....but if I CANNOT, will text. I am usually in turmoil inside, but I try not to show it. I love you but relationships scare me. In fact, I want to keep my identity even tho I'm not always thrilled with it. But even tho I'm not, I wouldn't want to be anyone else.

*Ha ha. A hot mess.
I love you...*

Subject: Re: Please Let Me Help
Date: 05/15/18 at 10:40:58 AM

My sweet Lisa ~ If you're willing, I'd like to chat more about our latest emails the next time I come for a stay --- hopefully on Friday --- but in the meantime, I have two comments on your last one now.

First, you should never feel that I've abandoned you when I go home because I'll always be back as long as you let me. Second, we're not going to have a meaningful relationship if you censor what you tell me. I won't head for the hills when you say whatever's on your mind and in your heart --- but I'll be very upset if you don't --- so please, please, PLEASE do that for both of our sakes!

On Wed, Jun 06, 2018 at 03:07 PM, Lisa wrote:

I've decided to stay in tonight...as much as I would (and always do) love to see you, I'm the Queen of Procrastination....so while I'm motivated, I need to get stuff done.

Please don't think it's because I would RATHER stay in. It isn't. Actually, I would RATHER find you in my bed so I can roll over and feel you next to me. I will hold that thought until you are here again.....that time will be here soon

Right now there are MUSTS and no rathers. I hope you enjoy McGill's (but not too much) .... do not, I repeat, do not sing sweet love songs to anyone else. You are the only person ever who sings to me and I love love love it...and you! You are quite wonderful and I'm not sharing.

"You're mine...and we belong together..."

Subject: I Love What You Say
Date: 06/06/18 at 07:25:58 PM

After getting your email and phone message, I just had to tell you again how much I always treasure your loving words. And even though we won't be together tonight, please think of me while you're packing and know I'm going to McGill's without you because I still have a good time with the other "regulars", but not nearly as good as when you join me because yes, baby doll ... I'm yours, and we <u>do</u> belong together . . . get some needed sleep and hopefully dream of us, my one and only love.

On Fri, Jun 15, 2018 at 04:58 PM, Lisa wrote:

Hi sweets...

Assuming you got home safe and sound.....
Looked for message, just saw your 'generic' one....hoping the romance isn't dead.? Yes, I'm too sensitive...but believe we should never take each other for granted.
Love you...

Subject: Don't Worry, Be Happy
Date: 06/15/18 at 06:24:01 PM

I'll never take you for granted, my dearest Lisa. I've just been very busy ever since I came home and didn't have a chance to write. You know that I love you and miss you terribly when I'm not there, but the visits do take a toll on my time, so I always have many, many things to do when I return home. I'll continue to be in a catch-up mode tonight, so this may be my last message until tomorrow. But I can't stand to be without you, so I'll just continue to do the best I can. Hope that's good enough, and that you have sweet dreams tonight ... of us.

On Jun 29, 2018 at 11:03 PM, Scott wrote:

My head is swimming after our telephone conversation because I'm not sure what happened. It may not be the best time to write to you when my mind is still in a fog, but against my better judgement, I'm going to do so anyway. Please forgive me if I ramble.

I know you're going through a very difficult time, and if my bringing up issues that I felt might make our staying together easier really did annoy you, then I apologize. You seemed to have good reasons for not pursuing them, but, of course, I didn't know what the reasons were before we chatted. And if you really think that my making those suggestions at all somehow meant that I don't love you enough, that makes me very sad.

I feel that I've fought very hard to keep you in my life, especially over the Joey situation, because I do love you dearly --- and always will --- and I believe that I've made many changes in my own life in order to do that. I'm not complaining. I made those changes willingly and, I believe, became much more flexible just to be with you. But I'm not sure I have enough fight left in me to keep trying to prove that to you if you keep questioning whether I love you enough for us to stay together and hang up on me as you did, even after I said that I'd stay over with you in your new home after you settle in to see how it goes.

If ending our conversation as you did means you don't want to see or talk with me again, then just let me know in a short email. I sincerely hope that's not what happens because it will break my heart, but if it does, then I'll accept your decision without question. But I hope after you think about it that you realize how deeply I do love you, and that being the case, would never try to intentionally destroy the truly wonderful relationship we have and make your life more difficult than it already is.

Subject: Re: My Thoughts
Date: 06/30/18 at 07:59:32 AM

My dearest Lisa ~   Based on the time you sent your email, it appears you had another restless night . . . as did I. I've inserted some underlined comments into your message below.

On Sat, Jun 30, 2018 at 12:06 AM, Lisa wrote:

Scotty. I did not hear you tell me you would see how it goes....what I heard was, it's too much trouble. I did say I'd give it a chance, but to be honest, I'm not optimistic about my having a great comfort level when I stay over because of a number of things --- e.g., the long drive to and fro, going up and down a flight of stairs many times each day and night to pee/shower/eat, sharing space with your P. and F. when I stay over and their feelings about that as well as mine, and the fact that my energy level is low due to my age, stress over our predicament, and worries about not having enough time at home to get everything done and enjoy it. But I'm not willing to have our relationship crash and burn if you're not.

It seemed that you were not willing to give it a chance. But I can accept your apprehension over the arrangements....maybe it won't work. However, I did say coming out to you more frequently may work.... As mentioned before, I'd like that. Let me know when you're ready to give it a try, even before you move or while you're still settling in if you'd like, and we'll decide what dates are good for both of us.

I think I am experiencing stress . I have no nails at all and I'm breaking out again.
Thus all came from out of the blue ....

It isn't what I chose. I'm not saying I'm sorry, I'm not. I would help them always. I'm glad I can. As am I. They need you now.

But every day, F. cries. She talks about B. because he's family to her. She wants to go home. P. cries too...imagine being 'home" one day, and practically homeless the next.

Maybe we should take a hiatus until things settle a bit. I have been irritable, on edge...and.sad
for them. I am not myself. Very argumentative I think. Edgy. Need understanding, not rules. You know I love you and that is a given...I like you too. Everything feels crazy right now. <u>I feel the same way. And it certainly wouldn't be a fair test of whether I'll be comfortable and happy staying over with you in your new environment until you move, settle in, make the place livable, and determine what things might be fun for us to do in that location.</u>

I fight to avoid becoming a cliché. And I don't necessarily disagree with what you said: I think

I didn't like the way you said it...... <u>You're right. I should have said some things differently or not at all. I'm very sorry about that.</u>

Enough for now. Will talk soon. <u>Okay . . . let's, as often as you feel the need, my darling Miss L.</u>

On Sat, Jun 30, 2018 at 05:51 PM, Lisa wrote:

I have been missing you, that's for sure. Your arms around me make me feel like the world is ok....that nothing bad could happen.
I don't know what the future holds for us. But living in the here and now is fine with me as long as you are in it.

On Wed, Jul 04, 2018 at 09:20 PM, Lisa wrote:

This love is real, is true, is exciting, is important .....I dream about you......I want you always in my life.....I long for you when you are not with me.

And that's how I feel my darling Scott

Subject: RE: You
Date: 07/04/18 at 09:56:55 PM

Your words just made my whole night, my whole week, my whole month, my whole year, and hopefully my whole life so very special and meaningful, my adorable Miss L. Thank you for being you. Sweet dreams, my dearest.

Subject: You and I and Everyone Else
Date: 07/15/18 at 08:13:16 AM

Didn't sleep well . . . exhausted . . . had a little breakfast, going back to bed. Still dizzy, but maybe somewhat better.

I'm uneasy and very sad about the unwanted changes in our lives --- your move and new living arrangements with F & P which will probably cut into our "alone" time --- my new health problems and the greater distance between us, making travel even harder than before --- having to sleep at T's place for now when I visit you --- no way to keep the heaven on earth exactly as we had it.

You seem to believe that our boundless love will carry us through. I hope you're right, but now, I'm just dazed and confused . . . and angry about circumstances in general . . . and we both know from our personal experiences that love doesn't always conquer all. Maybe this time it will. Time will tell.

Subject: Guess What?
Date: 07/15/18 at 02:50:03 PM

I've thought about our phone conversation, and you know what, my darling Lisa? I believe that our relationship is going to survive this latest hurdle and be stronger than ever.

I hope that you'll be patient with me if I feel like the odd man out right now, but it's killing me that I can't be close to you while everyone else dear to you can. Selfish? You bet. But I'm not going to apologize for wanting to be with my one and only love and envying those who are because they need you at this point in time. You should realize that I need you just as much as they do, and that's why I'm so sad.

You're a very strong and convincing woman, my dearest Miss L, and based on what you said, I'm certain that our time will come again quite soon.

On Sun, Jul 15, 2018 at 06:57 PM, Lisa wrote:

I am so glad you are on an upswing...and more optimistic. I just wish you were feeling better and hope going out is a positive thing.
Just..please...don't overdo it! I love you and want you around for the next chapter. I feel lucky to have found you and do NOT intend to let you go without a fight.....darlin', we will be together before you know it. Not soon enough, but it will happen!

You are the best!!!!!

On Wed, Aug 22, 2018 at 10:58 PM, Lisa wrote:

I wish I could adequately explain myself. Lately, I've been examining and reexamining my life. So many things I've done wrong. Blatantly wrong. So many feelings to sort and understand. I cry at the drop of a hat. I get angry in an instant. You get caught in the crossfire and I feel awful. Please understand. Maybe it has something to do with my milestone birthday. Don't know for sure.
I am feeling inadequate and a little lost.
We'll talk more. I love you, Scotty. Be patient.

Subject: An Early Morning Message
Date: 08/23/18 at 02:06:04 AM

I wish you wouldn't beat yourself up like you do. You're entitled to feel sad and cry from time to time . . . we all do. My shoulder will always be there for you. And we all make mistakes in our lives. You should leave those behind and just concentrate on what you did right, like rescuing P & F from a terrible situation and falling in love with me.

Yes, we'll talk more, and when we do, hopefully you'll realize what a truly wonderful woman you are and get rid of all those feelings of inadequacy. If you don't, I'll just have to spank you.

On Sat, Oct 06, 2018 at 06:38 PM, Lisa wrote:

I don't expect to hear from you tonight....but want you to know I am thinking about you......

Miss you baby
Can't hardly wait til vacation

Subject: RE: Hi sweets!
Date: 10/07/18 at 01:12:20 AM

I'm home now. McGill's was just okay --- not too many singers, so I was able to sing a half dozen or so tunes --- but it's never nearly as good as when you're by my side and I can serenade you. Why? So many reasons, but it all boils down to my endless love for you, baby doll. What a wonderful feeling!! Look forward to chatting with you on Sunday.

Chapter 5

Another Cliffhanger for the Relationship

* * * * * * *

Subject: My Afterthoughts About Last Night
Date: 10/26/18 at 09:38:20 AM

After our phone conversation last night, I had the feeling that I may never see nor hear from you again. You've made it clear that there are goals you want to pursue alone, but I believed there would always be room in your life for "us", no matter how full your plate is with other things.

The following excerpts from an email which I sent to you last January express my current thoughts, too. I've also included excerpts from your emails below as a reminder of what you said you felt for me this past year in the hope that, if you truly meant what you said, you'll realize how important we are to each other and therefore won't let our special romantic relationship crash and burn.

On Sat, Oct 27, 2018 at 10:34 AM, Lisa wrote:

It would be understated to tell you that you're a wonderful person...deserving of the best...now hurting....and I know I did this to you. I am so totally in pain these days....I guess I deserve it..... but I need to get my life in order. I have been blindsided with things I could not accept....and need to...and disgusted with my own actions. You deserve kindness and love. You deserve all good things. I cry a lot and feel it is depression and have to get past it. I crave breathing room and want to be alone and maybe through writing I can figure out who and what I am. I've gone about everything so wrong... I want to make it all right. Need some time.

Subject: RE: Your Last Message
Date: 10/27/18 at 12:44:38 PM

I can appreciate what you're trying to do, dear Lisa, and wanting time alone to get started. But my being without you completely is devastating and, I feel, unfair to both of us, especially since I love and miss you so much and firmly believe

I could help you through this crisis and ease your pain with comfort and support if you'd let me while you pursue your writing and other goals. I still think the way you're approaching this situation is a huge mistake --- i.e., excluding me from your life --- but, of course, it's your decision. Would it be possible, though, for you to give me any kind of estimate as to how much time you believe may pass before we'll see and talk with each other again and hopefully try to rekindle the wonderful relationship we had --- a week, a month, 6 months, a year, more? Having no idea about that is killing me!

Subject: A Suggestion Which I Hope You'll Life
Date: 10/28/18 at 08:30:11 AM

An idea popped into my head when I woke up this morning which, if you agree to give it a try, should help to ease the pain we're both feeling because we've been apart and bring us moments of joy together while at the same time ensuring that you currently have more than adequate "alone time" to define and start to work on your writings and other things you want to accomplish in your life.

I suggest that we get together for dinner at least once a month on a Friday to discuss the progress you've made toward attaining the goals you set, after which we could enjoy the karaoke session at The Oasis. You could then stay overnight at my place and head for home between noon and 1:00 on Saturday after we have lunch, which would give us time to continue our conversation from the night before and to keep the romance in whatever our relationship turns out to be in the future . . . if you feel the same, those stays could inspire us both by giving us the chance to continue all aspects of the relationship which has made our lives so meaningful.

If you agree that the above might be what we currently need to survive as a loving couple, I suggest that our first Friday get together be either November 9th or 16th. I'll be waiting with bated breath --- not gorilla breath --- to hear from you.

On Mon, Oct 29, 2018 at 07:07 PM, Lisa wrote:

Your suggestion is sound. But I am not quite there yet. I've been muddling through a lot of feelings and negativity...trying to get back on track. Slowly..surely...one foot in front of the other.....

I believe depression got me and I am shaking it off. Or trying to.
The source of some of it is how I treated you Scotty..I never wanted to hurt you but I did. I am not ready for a full blown relationship even though I miss you very much. Will I ever be?
I don't know. I cannot handle the responsibility now.

For the first time in my life I am being true to ME. And I'm not ready. You are the best...a wonderful man....a sweet soul. Who deserves more.
I hope we stay in touch. I know you must be angry.

Subject: Replying to Your Last Message . . .
Date: 10/29/18 at 10:29:19 PM

I understand and agree with most, if not all, of what you said, Lisa, especially the part where you said I deserve more. And what would that be? It would be the wonderful, loving woman I knew before --- the one who loved me, too, and who promised never to hurt me again. I need nothing less than that to inspire me to stay in touch. That doesn't mean having a relationship full of responsibilities --- just one in which we can love each other as a man loves a woman and a woman loves a man, even if it only involves getting together once a month or so for a couple of days to talk, have fun, etc. without interfering with your writing and pursuing other goals you decide are important in your life. What I don't need, and yes, what makes me angry, is for you to exclude me from your life altogether unless you plan to do that permanently.

I think it would be one of the biggest mistakes in both our lives --- and so unfair --- for you to do that. But if that's the case, please tell me and get it over with. Don't string me along with "maybe yes, maybe no". That's hurting me terribly right now, and perhaps that's one of the main reasons you're so depressed. Yes . . . you have to be true to yourself, but you seem to be convinced it's okay if that includes inflicting pain and suffering on me and perhaps others in the process. That's something I thought you'd never deliberately do to someone you love as much as you said you love me.

I know you want to leave some kind of legacy through accomplishments, but as I've said before, I hope someday you'll realize that you've already achieved one of the greatest goals for which a woman can strive --- being someone that a man like me, and your husband before me ---

can love and cherish. If I can't have that woman back, then I want to grieve for the heaven on earth I've lost for a time and then be alone forever . . . I'm begging you to decide as quickly as possible whether we can be together as we were before, even on a more limited basis, or need to go our separate ways to eventually stop the hurting that's gotten to be almost too much for me to bear.

On Sat, Nov 03, 2018 at 02:32 PM, Lisa wrote:

I read your msg...reread the one prior....I don't think you understand how you squeeze me to this point...where I cannot breathe or think and don't know what to do and can't shake off the anxiety . . . And I don't know what I want. But I can't function when you are doing the very thing I can't accept ...you are a terrific person Scott .....but you have a subtle way of leading me and right now it isn't good . . .

Subject: Re: Your Last Email
Date: 11/03/18 at 03:51:48 PM

I didn't mean to squeeze you, Lisa. Sorry it felt that way to you . . . I don't want to do anything to add to your anxiety.

On Thu, Nov 15, 2018 at 12:57 PM, Lisa wrote:

I started to msg you many times...but just couldn't. I have gone through numerous changes this month. I'm learning how to be on my own and deal with things myself. I really didn't know how, or forgot how.
I know I cannot be in a couples situation...not now...maybe never. I find I don't have enough to give someone and you, especially you, deserve a lot.
I always love you. This probably sounds odd to you but I do.
I'm changing the things about myself I don't like and trying to see some things the way you did....always positive. Always flattering. Always sure that I am nice. Well. I haven't felt so nice. Maybe this coming weekend we can talk? I owe you that and so much more.... If you don't want to I do understand. I breeched a trust and hurt you.
Let me know.

On Thu, Nov 15, 2018, at 3:02 PM, Scott wrote:

Yes, my dear Lisa, I <u>would</u> like to talk with you. I think we could have the most meaningful discussion if we did that face-to-face rather than over the phone. If you agree, we could meet for dinner and have that chat somewhere between our homes . . Let me know what you'd like to do.

On Thu, Nov 15, 2018 at 10:24 PM, Lisa wrote:

I have concerns...
If we meet..can we keep it friendly? No demands..no expectations?
Can we stay away from the blame game? I know you are angry..you must be.
I know that hurting you was awful....

You are a terrific man. I have no business being with anyone. I know this now.. more than ever.
Is this going to be too hard for us? Will we ever be able to be friends?
I don't know what to expect. I don't know what to say. I'm worried.
Dear Scotty.....I don't know how to make it better without compromising my life and dumping sadness in your lap.

Subject: Responding to Your Message
Date: 11/16/18 at 12:43:39 AM

In reply to your last email, Lisa, all I'd like for you to explain to me if you agree to meet is why you don't seem to want to keep me in your life at all other than perhaps as just a friend --- just a reminder that trying to do that would be too painful for me, as I've previously mentioned --- in view of the wonderful, romantic relationship we had, especially since we both still love each other so much.

Just to clarify my current thinking, you should know that all I'd need to prevent this from becoming the most devastating experience of my life is for us to keep the best aspects of our relationship intact by our getting together for a day or two every other month or so to be like we were before --- no strings, no demands, no expectations --- just being able to do a few of the things we both enjoy and to express our feelings for each other like we used to by holding hands, kissing, hugging and cuddling, making love, serenading each other at karaoke venues, etc. That's what you could do to make the situation better, something which I also believe wouldn't compromise your life and would certainly avoid dumping more sadness into my lap. I don't understand how that can possibly be too much to ask for considering the many ways you expressed your romantic love for me during this past year.

If you think it is, though, I'd like for you to give me specific reasons, preferably in person, as to why you're really ready to throw the baby out with the bath water, which to me would be one of the most foolish things you've ever done and something I suspect you'd regret some day when you realize the happiness we could have had. All I want is for us to be able to look forward to just a few fun and romantic times together again each year with someone we love. I don't see how that could possibly be anything but a meaningful and inspirational part of both our lives because I still believe you're terribly wrong when you say you have no business being with anyone. Continuing to be with me, even on the limited basis described above, can only be a good thing in my book, and I hope what I'm saying in this message makes you understand and appreciate the truth in that.

I don't know what else to say, and since I'm starting to ramble, I'll shut up and just ask that you consider discussing these issues further with me in whatever way you feel is best --- by email, by phone, or in person, with the last one being my preference. In the meantime, you still have my heart . . . and always will, which is why the thought of ending our romantic relationship is so horrible.

Chapter 6

Choosing the Right Path to Follow

* * * * * * *

On Sat, Nov 17, 2018, at 8:38 AM, Scott wrote:

I wanted to tell you again how overjoyed I am that we've been able to come up with a way to hopefully keep all of the good things about our relationship alive and flourishing while ensuring that our independence isn't compromised at all. You've made me so happy that my heart is ready to burst. I hope you feel the same.

On Sat, Nov 17, 2018 at 09:30 AM, Lisa wrote:

Scotty...what a sweet note....but it should read 'thanks to us.' I'm confident that things will work out and we will enjoy each other's company again....but in a way that allows us to be who we are.

*Being genuine...being true to oneself....is so important. Let's never compromise that again.
I have a feeling our time together will be extremely special.*

Let's start from this day forward ....today I'm feeling that fences are mended and all is right with the world. And I'm feeling that I'm lucky you are in my life! You are a sweet, kind man .....who else would try so hard to understand a kookoo bird like me?!

Love you dear S. It's a new day for us..

Subject: Re: My World Is Whole Again . . . Thanks to You Date: 11/17/18 at 11:09:17 AM

I agree with everything you said, my adorable Lisa, especially that we both need to be true to oneself. Without that, we can't be true to others.

I can't wait to see you and your lovely smile again on Tuesday! It's been much too long, you sweet kookoo bird.

Subject: I'm Home
Date: 11/20/18 at 02:59:00 PM

I made it home, safe and sound, with not too much additional back pain. Our being together again today was so very wonderful, and your hugs and kisses lifted me up to 7th Heaven. I hope you got a bit of a natural high from mine, too.

Talk to you soon, my one and only love . . .

On Tue, Nov 20, 2018 at 05:52 PM, Lisa wrote:

It was a truly magnificent day all around....
I was so happy to see you I wanted to burst! And the karaoke went very well with lots of participation.

Thank you again for surprising me with flowers! So thoughtful and sweet....they are really pretty!

So Scotty...again....was beyond happy to see you. Looking forward to next time......with love and kisses..

On Wed, Nov 21, 2018 at 10:36 PM, Lisa wrote:

I do remember the first time I went to Bohemia with you. I remember thinking that you are special, to bring music and joy there. They need it so much!

Plenty to be thankful for....

On 11/22/18 at 08:59:33 AM, Scott wrote:

I was very happy to hear that you remember the first time we hosted a Bohemia karaoke session together. I hope you'll keep the words which I wrote about that very special event in mind as a reminder of all the people who love you and whose lives you've touched and made so much better by your own loving and selfless words and deeds through the years --- especially me . . .

On Thu, Nov 22, 2018 at 10:00 AM, Lisa wrote:

I am happy you had a nice time yesterday... Will be thinking of you today and yes, we will plan more time together soon.
Got up a little while ago...fairly late...but had a restful sleep and it was nice. Today will come and go and then the Christmas frenzy begins.
I am seriously wondering about a venue....on the eve or Christmas day...where people are needed to

pitch in and help. I suppose but would be a better holiday if spent, at least part of the time, being useful. Just a thought.
I miss you today
But know we will be spending time together soon. Have been thankful for so much...and extremely hopeful.
It must be magic!
Love you dear Scotty

Subject: Your Lovely Thoughts
Date: 11/22/18 at 12:46:09 PM, Scott wrote:

Yes, my adorable Lisa, volunteering during the Christmas season is certainly a worthwhile thing to think about. You've inspired me to consider doing that, too, in addition to the Bohemia Christmas karaoke session and another one scheduled for Dec. 4th at the East Hampton Day Hab . . .

I'll be daydreaming about the next time we'll be together and being thankful for that.

Wishing you peace and magic.
You already have my heart.

On Thu, Nov 29, 2018, at 1:22 PM, Scott wrote:

I wanted to tell you again what a tremendous time I had yesterday and today with you. I'm more confident than ever that our relationship is indeed alive, healthy, and headed in the right direction. I'm soooooo happy that I'm still your man!

As promised, I've attached several of the pictures I took last year at the Smith Point holiday light show to give you and other folks you might want to bring along an idea of what it's like. I hope we can make it there this year --- should be fun.

I also hope to see you again soon, sweetheart. Let me know when that might be so I can start counting the hours.

On Thu, Nov 29, 2018 at 01:51 PM, Lisa wrote:

Oboy it was definitely terrific! Will plan another night out soon....in the meantime....just got home. (Thought about you...us...all the way home).... Smile

You are such a sweet and caring man, Scotty...
Feeling lucky
Happy
Content

Subject: Re: It Was Terrific !!!
Date: 11/29/18 at 02:22:22 PM

What nice sentiments, dearest Lisa. Your words will be on my mind, and in my heart, while I doze off for a nap in a few minutes. Call me later if you'd like, and remember, you're my one and only love, so I'm sharing those feelings with you.

Embracing Love in the Twilight Years

(Written by Lisa to Scott)

More ....
for you
the one who loves me
the one I love
the one who releases the real me
passion fills the air
you are all around me
even when you're not here.

My promise to you ---
to love you thru thick and thin
to always tell you what I'm thinking
to consider your feelings
to tell you how important you are
    to me .... and to the world

Plenty to be thankful for ....
Family, friends, special friends ....
A special friend .... you ....
    although you are much much more.

Whomever in the universe I should thank ....
　　well, thanks!!!!
Life is good.

Feeling lucky today, for many reasons ....
I have you in my life and have your love.
How could it be any better?
I have kids and grandkids I love.
Granted, the road is rocky at times ....
　　but at the end of the day the love is intact!
I have friends I adore and trust.
They are good people and
　　I am fortunate to know them.
I have some relatives who have weathered
　　the storms with me.

So all in all .... life is good.
I HAVE come through some hard times ....
　　but I also know it is much worse for some.
When our paths cross, I will try to make their
　　lives easier.

You show me every day that we have everything
　　because we have each other....
You are one of my many blessings.

Editor's Epilogue

The Key to Staying Alive

* * * * * * *

The moral of this story is that it's never too late for romance to come into two people's lives, but love isn't always enough to keep any relationship from crashing and burning. Therefore, to help ensure its survival, you should also respect your loved one's wants and needs, just as both Lisa and Scott have vowed to do in the hope that this pledge will enable them to be a meaningful and inspirational part of each other's world for a long time to come.

As we bid adieu to our loving couple, Catherine Mayrides provides us with an appropriate ending to this chronicle with her poetic verses that touch on the type of feelings which Lisa and Scott may be savoring at this very moment.

My darling Scott . . .
Sometimes . . .
I want to hold onto you
    and disappear in your arms,
Contemplating my good fortune

at being important to you.

You mean the world . . .
You deserve the world!
I would give it to you if I could,
But I can only offer
    Myself, My truth, My love.
Hold onto me . . .

Dearest Lisa . . .
The room lights up
    when you walk in
And music plays somewhere,
Filtering into my reality,
Completing my happiness,
Reminding me that I am worthy,
That I deserve this . . .
That I'm loved and I can love.
The world lights up!

www.ingramcontent.com/pod-product-compliance
Lightning Source LLC
Chambersburg PA
CBHW072159160426
43197CB00012B/2452